WRITE SOURCE®

GREAT SOURCE EDUCATION GROUP

a Houghton Mifflin Company
Wilmington, Massachusetts

Written and Compiled by
Carol Elsholz, Patrick Sebranek,
and **Dave Kemper**

Illustrated by **Chris Krenzke**

Acknowledgements

We're grateful to many people who helped bring *The Writing Spot* to life. First, we must thank all the teachers and students from across the country who contributed their ideas. Also, a special thanks to the following teachers who helped make this book a reality.

Debbie Bowman   Julie Los   Connie Olsen
Deb Caldwell   Dian Lynch   Randy Rehberg
Maureen Gebhardt   Lisa Mosier   Amy Ricketts

Finally, we want to thank our Write Source/Great Source team for their help: Laura Bachman, Colleen Belmont, Sandra Easton, Sherry Gordon, Lois Krenzke, Ellen Leitheusser, Tina Miller, Sue Paro, Richard Spencer, and Sandy Wagner.

Dear Students,

The Writing Spot is a book about writing. We wrote this book just for you. It will help you write better and have fun at the same time.

We hope you like it.

Your friends at the Write Source

P.S. Be sure to look for Spot. He likes to read and write, and he does a lot of funny things, too!

Table of Contents

I have a special writing spot.
     It's where I **look**
          and **think** a lot.

It's where I **talk** and **listen**, too,
     and where I **read**
          of things brand-new.

But most of all, when I am there,
     I **write** and draw, and then I **share**.

Spot writes.

4

Writers look and think.

Writers read.

Writers write.

Writers share.

We send notes and cards.

10

We make lists.

We write in journals.

It was A sunny, funny day. THE fox was singing, and A bear was dancing.
OLIVIA

We tell and write stories.

We make signs.

We use computers to write.

15

We work and play together.

16

Aa alligator
Bb butterfly
Cc cup
Dd duck
Ee eggs
Ff fish

Gg girl
Hh hat
Ii igloo
Jj jacket
Kk kite
Ll ladybug
Mm mouse

Nn nest
Oo octopus
Pp penguin
Qq quilt
Rr rocket
Ss socks

Tt turtle
Uu umbrella
Vv vase
Ww wagon
Xx box
Yy yarn
Zz zipper

Writers explore letters, sounds, and words.

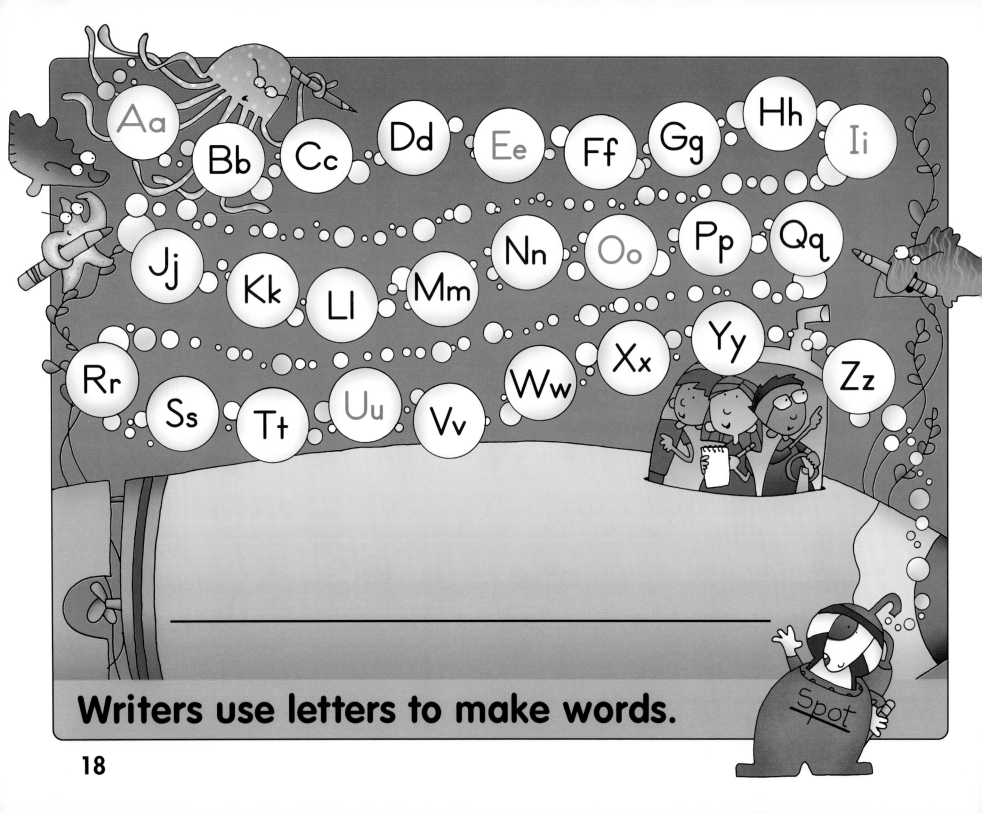

Writers use letters to make words.

_____Spot_____ puts words together.

I like to write.
_____

_____ puts words together.

_____

_____ puts words together.

_____

Writers put words together in sentences.

19

Alligator sits,
Butterfly flits.

Igloo white,
Jacket bright.

Cup of tea,
Duck at sea.

Kite in the sky,
Ladybug shy.

Eggs to cook,
Fish in a brook.

Mouse near a hole,
Nest like a bowl.

Girl named Mary,
Hat for Harry.

Alligator to . . .